# IS IT OVERCROWDED IN HEAVEN?

# IS IT OVERCROWDED IN HEAVEN?

### FRAN LANDESMAN

**GOLDEN HANDSHAKE**
LONDON

First published in 1981 by
Jay Landesman Limited
159 Wardour Street
London W1

© Fran Landesman 1981

Golden Handshake is an imprint
of Jay Landesman Limited

ISBN 0 905150 38 4

Printed in Great Britain by The Anchor Press Ltd
and bound by Wm Brendon & Son both of Tiptree, Essex.

# CONTENTS

## I  FAMILY AFFAIRS

## II TANGLED ROMANCES

## III  URBAN REFLECTIONS

5

## IV LIFE ON THE RACK

## V ULTIMATE ISSUES

# I
# FAMILY AFFAIRS

# MOTHER

M is for my masochistic urges
O is for the ordeals I endure
T is for the tear-drop that emerges
H is for my line of horse manure
E is for my poor deflated ego
R is for the rotten life I've led

Put them altogether they spell
                MOTHER
The woman who fucked up my head

# REMEMBER ME?

Remember me from Holy Redeemer High
The girl with her feet in the aisle and her head in the sky
Miss King, the English teacher said
My essays were the best
But after all the books I read
I flunked the final test

Time passed like pain at Holy Redeemer High
Most of the sisters were teaching us not to fly
My cousin Ann became a nun
Rose Mary's at the store
And I remember you alright
Your seat was near the door

You were one of the popular girls
In a white angora sweater
My Aunty June would have bought me one
But my mother wouldn't let her
'It will only turn her head
And you know the way they shed,' she said

The clumsy one who couldn't play games was me
You shone in the circle of light where I wanted to be
I recognised you right away
You haven't changed a bit
I know I've gained a lot of weight
But all I do is knit
I stay at home with Daddy and watch him die
Remember me from Holy Redeemer High

# HOME

Home is where you hang your hat
And can't get a break
Home is what you ought to want
But can't really make

Home is where you're always wrong
Too fat or too thin
Home's an endless argument
You never can win

Home is a test you always fail
Emotions you have to fake
Where everybody does his thing
For somebody else's sake

Home is where love's old sweet song
Just won't set you free
Home is where you're not the way
They want you to be

Home sweet home will haunt your dreams
Wherever you go
Home is what there's no place like
But didn't you know
Home is where the heartache
Really started

# DO A DANCE FOR DADDY (II Chorus)

Do a dance for Daddy
In a satin gown
It's a celebration
When he comes to town
Do a dance for Daddy
Show him he's the boss
Give him all your power and never count the loss

When he's feeling weary
Wash your Daddy's feet
Smother all your anger
Keep your temper sweet
Ask for his permission
When you've got a plan
If you have a problem just take it to the man

Write a book for Daddy
Learn to cook for Daddy
Play the flute for Daddy
Cut up cute for Daddy

Entertain your Daddy
Always play his game
If you're just a shadow
Daddy's not to blame
Daddy is your teacher
Critic, Christ and friend
You do it all for Daddy but you hate him in the end

Look your best for Daddy
Pass your test for Daddy
Stand up tall for Daddy
Do it all for Daddy

# SONG OF SHAKESPEARE'S SISTER

If Shakespeare had had a sweet sister
As wonderfully gifted as well
They'd have given her no chance of learning
Her genius would make her life hell
Betrothed to be wed by her father
Before she was out of her teens
She'd cry out that marriage was hateful
Face beatings and terrible scenes
She'd then take the high road to London
And stand by the stage door like him
Ambitious to start as an actress
They'd laugh at her lunatic whim
She'd never have gotten a training
Though her mind teemed with unwritten plays
And her fancy was quick as her brothers
Folk would think such a young woman crazed
When her plight roused some actor to pity
She'd be very soon gotten with child
So she'd kill herself one winter morning
For her fate would have driven her wild
If Shakespeare had had a bright sister
She'd have met with derision not praise
She might have been martyred for witchcraft
She'd never have written the plays

## JUST ALONG FOR THE RIDE

Used to be I was just along for the ride
In the snapshots a smiling face at your side
Mr Big Shot's a wee bit bored little bride
Just along for the ride

Home from work you expected me on my knees
Drinking scotch you were distant and hard to please
Wife and mother, I always felt ill at ease
I kept losing my keys

Now here I am at that terrible age
When women surrender to boredom and rage
Suddenly feeling this isn't the end
And you, my old jailer, are more like a friend

Used to be I would dream about suicide
Now I write about feelings I used to hide
If I blow it at least they'll know that I tried
And I'm not anybody
Just along for the ride

# THE UNRULY MISTRESS

You come to me complaining about your mistress
You tell me she's become a nagging wife
The lady that you said
Was fabulous in bed
And brought such sauce and sunshine to your life

You say she's got the bad taste to criticise you
She makes demands, she cavils and complains
She isn't satisfied with polishing your pride
And keeping your self image free from stains

Well, I know all about you dear
Your boredom and your glory
And I must say I'd like to hear
Miss Pamela's side of the story

You come to me complaining about your mistress
Her lack of tact has cut you like a knife
While I stay safe at home
And write this little poem
And play the part of understanding wife

# DIVORCE

I always knew
I ought to get a divorce
Everyone has them
How can I be a paid-up member
Of the modern movement
Married thirty years to the same man

I would have looked so good
On the witness stand
In an elegant understated outfit
My hand on the Bible
The only sticky bit
Would be going home
Without you

# SIAMESE TWINS

You're never alone when you're a Siamese twin
There's someone to share the situation you're in
There's somebody there each time you lose or you win
You're never alone when you're a Siamese twin

We don't exclude coition
Sometimes we like a bit
To find the right position
Is a challenge we admit

If you don't want to make it
There's always an excuse
You never have to fake it
With a twin as a caboose

Each time we get down to it
We think of something new
Of course it's hard to do it
Like the missionaries do

When roused to passion we may
Indulge in fancy sin
You've always got a three-way
When you're a Siamese twin

So don't feel sorry for us
We've got no cause to moan
Our lovers never bore us
'Cause we've got our funny bone

# II
# TANGLED ROMANCES

# COME HERE, GO AWAY

Come here, go away
That is what I hear you say
Hold me tight but let me stray
I don't fancy it today

Come here, go away
Learn what signals to obey
Now I want you. Now I don't
Now I'll kiss you. Now I won't

Please tell me what you really think
No, never mind I want a drink
You're looking wonderful tonight
What makes you think you're always right

Love me now and then
There's no way of knowing when
It will be your lucky day
We'll call you when it's O.K.

Love dies, love is made
Feeling makes us feel afraid
Please don't touch me
Now you may
Come here
Go away

# MORNING SONG

He comes to see her in the morning
When the sun shines on her bed
The sheets are scented by her body
And the dreams still in her head

At first he crawls in bed beside her
And they lie there still as spoons
And then his fingers touch her body
Till he finds familiar tunes

Sometimes they spend the day together
And sometimes it's love and run
He comes with other little blessings
Like the milk, the mail, the sun

He sees her early in the morning
With the sleep still in her eyes
He puts a pillow underneath her
And they find the way to paradise

# SHOES

I don't know why I let you stay
But I just can't refuse
We have a smoke and right away
You're taking off your shoes

You haven't got a word to say
No gossip, jokes or news
I mention it's a rainy day
You're taking off your shoes

This isn't what you'd call romance
We tell no tender lies
I never even get a chance
To look into your eyes

The love we make is cold as death
It's not what I would choose
Before I even catch my breath
You're putting on your shoes

I wish that you would stay and eat
Or have a little talk
But you just knock me off my feet
And then you take a walk

Our crazy loving goes so fast
You've got no time to lose
I try to make the moment last
You're putting on your shoes

# WISHFUL THINKING

When the dust has finally settled
When you come in for a landing
As your taxi leaves the airport
When you get to where you're going
With an ocean in between us
Do you think perhaps you'll miss me?

Will you find that I have some redeeming features
Will your days with me be pleasant to recall
Will you finally see my virtues in perspective
And decide maybe you love me after all

When you've finished your unpacking
And you've sorted out your memories
As the days go on unfolding
And you're drinking with your buddies
With an ocean in between us
Do you think perhaps you'll miss me?

Will you wake up one fine morning and discover
It was me you really wanted from the start
Will you wish that I was lying there beside you
And be sorry that you broke my tender heart
When there's time to think it over
With an ocean in between us
Will you suddenly discover
That you miss me?

# SO IT GOES

I ask if you love me
And are you fond of me
That goes without saying
You always say

You simply amaze me
Whenever you praise me
'Cause you're just not playing
The game that way

I wish you'd say something
Just any old dumb thing
Inferring you fancy
My art or my toes

There's no way of knowing
Just what keeps it going
It goes without saying
But still it goes

# DO YOU REALLY FEEL FREE

You come home early from the party
It was too much like working you said
An effort making conversation
You'd much rather be here with me on the bed

You make me think I understand you
And I'm making a map of your head
You tell me about all your lovers
The edge of the knife sort of life that you've led

And you find the world quite taxing
But it seems like you're relaxing
And it seems to me the pieces really fit
And I think I've touched the real you
And I think that I can heal you
And we have a lot of laughs you must admit

Outside this room the world is waiting
All the hustle and hype that you fled
But honey, what I want to know is
Do you really feel free here with me on this bed

Is it less like work
Is it more like play
Does it come for free
Do we have to pay
And how do I know how you feel
And how do I know what is real

# YOU MAKE ME SO NERVOUS

You make me so nervous
You make me so tense
I snap and I stammer
It doesn't make sense

You make me so nervous
I talk much too fast
And when we're both happy
I'm scared it won't last

The pleasure you give me at moments
Is more than my pen can express
But why do you give me the feeling
That I'm such a terrible mess

When you're in a bad mood
You make me so sad
I simply can't bear it
You're driving me mad

But all of my worries
Dissolve when we touch
You make me so nervous
I love you so much

# LITTLE OLD LOVE-MAKER YOU

There's a lady in London who loves you
There's a Lord and a sailor or two
And some talented girls who are tearing their curls
Over little old love-maker you

I am sure you must charm the gorilla
And the seals when you visit the zoo
The smooth and the rough simply can't get enough
Of little old love-maker you

And even I have fallen, who once stayed so aloof
The thought of you affects me like rolling off a roof

You have lovers all over Manhattan
They don't do you much good it is true
You seduce everyone but it isn't much fun
For little old love-maker you

There's a lady in London who loves you
And a cat and a budgie or two
And even a goat who is slitting his throat
Over little old love-maker you

# HAPPY NEW YEAR

I'm feeling cool and collected
Facing another New Year
All of the prospects are pleasing
Skies are beginning to clear

Maybe I miss you a little
Maybe I wish you were here
Still I'm not killing the hours
Waiting for you to appear

You were my fantasy lover
You were the thorn in my side
Now that such pleasures are over
Thanks for a wonderful ride

Sometimes I'll catch myself sighing
Saying your name with a curse
But I've got one consolation
Your week is bound to be worse

Really I'm feeling much better
I've shed my last bitter tear
Though I don't fancy your chances
I wish you a Happy New Year

# III
# URBAN REFLECTIONS

# CITY SONG

I'm not a nature poet. I sing a city song
Green fields do not enchant me
That's not where I belong
And when it comes to gardens why should I break my neck
I'd rather ride the subway
Besides my thumb is black

At night your country squire collapses in a heap
They start in snoring early
And I can't get to sleep
The cricket's song at sundown just orchestrates my blues
And I don't want to wake up
To cock-a-doodle-doos

You will never catch me camping in the country
Getting bitten in a dell or leafy thicket
You'll find me and my gent dancing on the cement
Every time I see a tree I want to kick it

Mine is a city story. Won't give you any hype
About the joys of nature
'Cause I'm an urban type
Can't fake it in the country, the days are far too long
The life is far too wholesome
I miss the city's song

# I'M SUPPOSED TO BE IN SOHO

I'm supposed to be in Soho
One half an hour ago
I'm supposed to meet some people
With a half an ounce of snow

I've been trying hard to leave you
Didn't mean to stay so long
But I'll have another brandy
And I'll sing just one more song

I wish that I were one of those
Who says he's going and then he goes
But every time I say goodbye
The flow gets going and hours fly

If I leave it any later
They'll be moving on from there
And I know I ought to call them
But I'm anchored to this chair

They're expecting me in Soho
Not to show up would be wrong
But I'll have another brandy
And I'll sing just one more song

# YOUR MACHINE

Sitting in the airport all alone
I felt I had to call you on the phone
I only got to talk to your machine
I tried to keep the message short and clean

I'm sure I must have sounded quite absurd
I know I didn't say the magic word
Time up I put the phone down with regret
I haven't learned to do it smoothly yet

To leave a message by machine
Is really quite an art
Your voice comes on and then the beep
And then it's time to start
It's hard to get the words out
Through the pounding of my heart

I never seem to say just what I mean
I'm tempted to be flippant or obscene
When panic trips my tongue I want to shout
Because I know that time is running out

I'm not so good at playing farewell scenes
And it makes me crazy
Talking to machines

# FRIENDS

There are friends that you grow up with
There are friends you make at school
There's the kid who's kinda crazy
And the one who plays it cool
There are cronies and companions
Mere acquaintances and mates
There are friends who made you giggle
When you went on double dates

There are friends you love to hear from
There are some whose calls you dread
There are friends who share your traumas
There are friends for whom you've bled
There are friends who are successful
There are friends who cannot cope
There are friends who bake you cookies
There are friends who smoke your dope

There are friends who ring your doorbell
When you want to be alone
There are friends who never hang up
When they get you on the phone
I've had gay friends come what may friends
Some OD'ed and wound up dead
But the best as I remember were the ones I found in bed

There are friends who just amuse you
There are old relationships
There are friends who try to use you
There are pals who give you tips
There are friends who get so heavy
That their words are made of lead
There are friends who have to tell you
What another friend has said

There are friendships that develop
When you're working on a show
There are beach pals. There are ski pals

There are friendships built on snow
There are friends who steal your husband
There are friends who screw your wife
There are friends who spend the weekend
There are friends who change your life

There are eyes you fall right into
Where the loving never ends
And we recognise these people
As the treasures we call friends.

# TANGIERS NEW YEAR

The moon of Tangiers
Is a tangerine
It swims in the sky
Like a silver queen

The hash of Tangiers
Is a feather bed
It smothers the shit
That fucks up your head

The lord of the house
Is a man of style
He enters a room
And he makes you smile

We try to connect
As the New Year nears
While blindly observed
By the moon of Tangiers

# LAMENT FOR SEAN

I heard that you died somewhere in Spain
Another refugee from London rain
We didn't see each other much before it happened
Now I don't know why I want to cry
You were always such a reckless guy
Oh Sean, I'm sorry that you're gone

You got into an awful wreck
On the road back from the discotheque
It was a shock when someone showed me where it
    happened
You used to be an instant high
But you were always such a reckless guy
Oh Sean, I'm sorry that you're gone

You were the last of the head-band wearing hippies
Macho moustache and an earring made of gold
'Zorro Lives' was hand embroidered on your jacket
But your eyes were on the edge of growing old

This island is a crazy place
The people come from outer space
They say you had a feeling something might go
    wrong here
And so you came to Spain to die
You were always such a reckless guy
Oh Sean, I'm sorry that you're gone

I think your ghost is still floating round Ibiza
I can see you getting pissed in Sandy's Bar
I wish we could have said goodbye
You were always such a reckless guy
So long Sean, I hope you like this song
Goodbye Sean, farewell Sean

# CRYING WOLFE

I've just read a book by Tom Wolfe, *In Our Time*
He makes me feel like I've committed a crime
The text and the drawings are savage and grim
I hope that I won't ever run into him

He'd hate what I say and he'd hate what I wear
He'd jeer at my house, he'd sneer at my hair
I've reached middle age which to Tom is a sin
I've studied his book and I know I can't win

I'd love to know who his heroes are
I'd like to know who he digs
'Cause his pen condemns the human race
As a hideous breed of pigs

He's brutal to women, he's murder on men
The working class ape and the middle class hen
He chides their pretensions, chastises each pose
The main thing he cannot forgive is their clothes

He may be a perfect sweetie-pie
His heart may be purest gold
He looks kinda cute in his sharp white suit
But his book makes my blood run cold

He mocks at the middle, he scorns the extremes
He's hard on their habits, he scoffs at their dreams
My style may be awful, my soul may be jive
But thank goodness Tom Wolfe doesn't know I'm alive

# THE USUAL

I wake up alone every morning
Awash with the usual pain
I stare at the window and what do I see?
The usual London rain

I leave right on time for the office
And wait for the usual train
What is it that weeps down the back of my neck?
The usual London rain

The usual lunch in the usual pub
Is as tasteless as ever it was
I wish that somebody would buy me a drink
But as usual nobody does

I go to the usual party
And pick up a typist called Jane
And what makes us hurry to get to her flat?
The usual London rain

I go through the usual motions
Pretending to be Michael Caine
And what do I hear when she turns out the light?
The usual London rain

# IF THEY CAN'T TAKE A JOKE

I'm not really much of a singer
I try for a high note and croak
The critics may give me the finger
But fuck 'em if they can't take a joke

My act is obscene and offensive
I once made a publisher choke
They can't put me on the defensive
Fuck 'em if they can't take a joke

True to myself and toujours gay
That's how I am, that's how I'll stay
Sometimes I fly sometimes I fall
But like they say — you can't win 'em all

My love life has been a fiasco
The last was a working-class bloke
I sprinkled his balls with tabasco
But fuck him if he can't take a joke

I've noticed that people are staring
My lyrics disgust decent folk
But my motto is always be daring
And fuck 'em if they can't take a joke

# IV
# LIFE ON THE RACK

# LIFE ON THE RACK

Life on the rack
The monkey on your back
You thought you were an artist
But now you're just a hack

Sundays are black
When living on the rack
You bought some new equipment
And then you got the sack

Aside from your personal crisis
The world is in terrible shape
You hustle to pay for your vices
'Cause everyone needs an escape

Life on the rack
Your lover won't come back
You miss those sweet encounters
It seems you've lost the knack
Love, money and self-confidence
And little things you lack
Just grin and bear it, Mac
You're living on the rack

# SPARKS

Sparks — from too many cigarettes
Left holes in my favourite dress
Left holes in the blanket
But we had a good time

Now — alone with my cigarettes
Just look at this awful mess
These holes in the blanket
These burns on my mind

You did me some fantastic turns
But now that you're gone old lover of mine
I spy all these unsightly burns
And how can I fit them into a rhyme

Now — it seems that my world's in holes
I'm sick of my Russian soul
I feel like I'm choking
And I wish I had the strength
To give up smoking

# DAYDREAM AT THE DENTIST

I've got a hole in my soul
Sometimes it hurts like hell
For a while it felt better
With you inside me
But that was only
A temporary filling

# THE TIGERS OF PAIN

The tigers of pain
Prowl out in the rain
Not far from the circle of light
Behind our locked doors
Their passionate roars
Assault us by day and by night

The famines and wars
On faraway shores
Send echoes that batter your heart
There's fire and flood
And spilling of blood
You wait for your troubles to start

When love comes along
Your head's full of song
It's hard to stay sober and sane
But be on your guard
For out in the yard
Are the terrible tigers of pain

# CRYING TO GET OUT

Inside every fat girl
There's a thin girl crying to get out
Sweet and sad and slinky
That nobody ever knows about

Inside every old man
There's a young man crying to get out
Just behind the wrinkles
Is the kid who used to twist and shout

It's the envelope that lies
Only look into their eyes
See the lonely dreamers there
Building castles in the air

Inside every hater
There's a lover dying of the drought
Inside every killer
There's a lover crying to get out
Trying to get out
Dying to get out
All the locked up lovers
Crying to get out

# IF FOOD DIDN'T MAKE YOU FAT

I simply can't help complaining
I constantly sing the blues
It seems like it's always raining
My feet never fit my shoes
It isn't beyond God's power
To cheer up my habitat
Life wouldn't be half so sour
If food didn't make you fat

I could get such joy from eating
Except for the pinch of guilt
The whisper that says "you're cheating!"
It must be the way I'm built
It's easy to chase a trouble
With nibbles of this and that
My happiness count would double
If food didn't make you fat

Or else I could pass the hours
Adored by some gentle lad
My path would be strewn with flowers
If love always left you glad
But love, though it's not nutritious
Can easily drive you mad
This life would be so delicious
If love didn't make you sad

Some think I'm a lucky sinner
Successful and worldly wise
Sometimes I may back a winner
Sometimes I may win a prize
But somehow it seems I never
Get quite what I'm aiming at
I think I could eat forever
If food didn't make you fat

# SADIE-MAY PLAY

Master and slave, master and slave
Give us a taste of the lash that we crave
Everyone's playing from cradle to grave
We all misbehave

Pleasure and pain, pleasure and pain
Playing with fire, the whip and the chain
Is there a secret locked up in my brain?
Let's bring back the cane

Destruction used to be my aim
Now I'm sick of it
It takes two fools to play this game
And I want to quit

User and used, user and used
I play the victim, betrayed and abused
Let's stop the game, I'm no longer amused
And I don't want to play
Not today anyway

# THE VACANT HEART

Two ten milligram valium to fall asleep at dawn
Lying in bed on a Saturday with the TV on
Its *The Magnificent Seven* with the younger
    Steve McQueen
Don't remember last night at all, just can't recall
    the scene
Vacant heart, hand and eye
Easy live, easy die
The sheets are stained with make-up and vaseline
But Steve McQueen is young again on the screen

One o'clock in the afternoon. The sky's like lead
Guess I'm one of the lucky ones, I can stay in bed
Phone rings but I don't answer it. There's no one left
    to call
I really give a damn about. There's not much left at all
Vacant heart, hand and eye
Easy live, easy die
I've used up my resources and the slate's not clean
But Steve McQueen is young again on the screen

Maggie died a year ago. We stayed in touch
I keep trying to tell myself it didn't matter much
I don't really understand her death or how it came
The games we played were dangerous. I don't know
    who  to blame
And I'm not even certain my own hands are clean
But Steve McQueen is young again on the screen
Vacant heart, hand and eye
Easy live, easy die
I think I'll stay in bed. I'm just a stalled machine
But Steve McQueen is young again on the screen
Yes, Steve McQueen is young again on the screen

# WHITE BOY SINGING THE BLUES

I'm just a white boy singing the blues
A poor up-tight boy singing the blues
I don't start any riot
I don't get on TV
I'm sober clean and quiet
So nobody cheers for me

I'm just a white boy singing the blues
The troubles I got don't make the news
I'm not a Jew or Nigger
Though I love rock 'n' roll.
I've never pulled a trigger
So they say I ain't got soul

Everybody's heroes get busted now and then
But I just can't be trusted 'cause I ain't been in the pen

I'm just a blue boy sore at the blacks
The good Lord gives them shit that I lacks
They dance and play and brawl best
They sing the truest songs
Of course those boogies ball best
'Cause they've got the biggest dongs

I'm just a white boy singing the blues
Alone at night boy singing the blues
A poor up-tight boy singing the blues
About a white boy singing the blues

# PORTRAIT OF NOBODY

On your desk there's a picture of nobody
And nobody calls you on the phone
You make plans to have dinner with nobody
You wake up and find that you're alone

Once your hours were crowded with somebodies
They played Space Invaders with your heart
Now you reach out for no one and nobody
And nothing is tearing you apart

No matter how you tried
No one was satisfied
They threatened suicide
To stay beside you
Now there is no one home
Inside your pleasure dome
And you no longer roam with love to guide you

You are matched up and married to nobody
You've driven the lovers from your life
There is only the ghost of a melody
The memory of someone else's wife

You return the affections of nobody
And nobody's stories make you yawn
You explain your departures to nobody
And nobody will notice when you're gone

# WHY SHOULD LOVE BE SO HARD ON THE HEART

Why should love be so hard on the heart
Why does it caress you then tear you apart
Why does it fool you, why does it tease you
Why does it scare you, why does it please you

Why should love be so loaded with pain
Why does it betray you again and again
Why does the promise fade so unfairly
Why does the magic happen so rarely

Ah, those wonderful wild men
They hammer your heart like a fist
You spend your time yearning and sighing and burning
While they're always out getting pissed

Why should love be so tied up in knots
Well either it's that or it's making cheap shots
It gives us a kick and inspires our art
But why should love be so hard on the heart

Times are changing they tell us
There must be a new way to live
Alongside a new love, a tender and true love
Who'll gladly return what we give

Why should love be so much on the mind
It staggers our senses and makes us all blind
There must be an answer, we're all so damn smart
So why should love be so hard on the heart

# V
# ULTIMATE ISSUES

# IS IT OVERCROWDED IN HEAVEN?

Is it overcrowded in heaven
Are they standing in line to get in
Well just think of the innocent children
Snuffed, before they committed one sin

All the sheriffs and teachers and judges
Never break any one of God's laws
And those wonderful radio preachers
Must be Christians without any flaws

There's no place for promiscuous cuties
Or the guy with a spoon up his nose
Just the sane and the saved and the sinless
Do you think there are millions of those?

Is it overcrowded in heaven
With no sign of a Buddhist or Jew
I'm sure that poor Jesus gets lonely
And he's keeping a welcome for you

Do you think that maybe it's boring
And there's nothing much doing at night
Well at least you're not burning or boiling
And your neighbours are all lily white

Is it overcrowded in heaven
Down on earth things are just a bit grim
And while God's forgiving the sinners
Does he wonder if we'll forgive him

## SO REAL

Big fat lady
Jumping up and down with joy
'I just saw my favourite star
From a television show
Walking down the street

I had nothing for him to sign
But the lining of my coat'
She said displaying his autograph
'My daughter will flip
He was walking down the street
The one from the Doctor show
You know
Wearing a blue suit
He seemed so real'

And I thought
That's why we want to be stars
So we can walk down the street
And dazzle the people
Giving them instant pleasure
And we won't have any aches at all
Because we'll only seem to be real

## DON'T DO IT MY WAY

Do it his way do it your way
If you're looking for a sure way
Do it her way do it their way
Try the hip way or the square way
Leave it open leave it shut
Follow any passion but
Don't do it my way

Do it that way do it some way
You can make it any dumb way
There are problems and solutions
(Also mental institutions)
Play it hot or play it cool
If you want to play the fool
Then do it my way

We saw eye to eye
We always got along
You agreed with me
And we were always wrong
So baby

Try to make it on the highway
Or the safe way or the sly way
Try the castles in the sky way
Or the honest do-or-die way
But you never will succeed
If you follow where I lead
Everyone will say you blew it
If you're dumb enough to do it
My way
Don't do it my way

# NOTHING SHALL BE GIVEN

Nothing shall be given to the needy
The needy and the greedy shall be lost
As long as you don't need it you can have it
Don't add it up or think about the cost

Don't think that someone's out there who can fix it
A lover who will cover every need
Everyone will shun you when you're hungry
'Cause no one wants a friend they have to feed

I know how to show you the way
Though I'm just as hopeless as you
So try hard to do what I say
But don't ever do as I do

Anyone who's looking for a handout
Will find that life is biased toward the strong
And even when they get it they can't hold it
'Cause nothing ever lasts for very long
And that includes this dull depressing song

# ME

I don't want to be a woman
I don't want to be a man
I don't want to be a Jew
Or a Presbyterian
I don't want to be an American
I don't want to be French

I want to be an androgynous time traveller
Stopping off for a coffee
Dropping off in the arms of a stranger
With an ancient earring
And a crooked smile
Who tells me I remind him
Of some lover he left on Venus

# THE RIGHT TO HAPPINESS

Americans believe they are entitled to happiness
That's why they're all so sad and lonely it seems
They haven't got much time to waste, they're up and
   they're doing things
Pursuing their intense American dreams

In forty years, give or take a few springs
They only have time for occasional flings
Then they feel cheated by God up above
Who gave them a garden and promised them love

Americans have homes just like the ones in the magazines
Or if they don't they just can't hold up their heads
They have to get a road map from a priest or psychiatrist
To cross the desert of their over-sized beds

To cure their blues they go shopping for things
That never come wrapped up in paper and strings
It seems the Big Apple is black at the core
And no one finds gold in the street any more

Americans believe they must be handsome and popular
And if they're not they're filled with doubt and despair
They chase their dreams in monster cars and crack up
   in Disneyland
Or tear out all their newly transplanted hair
And the old folks dream of the way it used to be
When happiness was their manifest destiny
And the boys and girls run away to God or drugs
While the Statue of Liberty watches the sea and shrugs

# SORRY BOBBY

I'm sorry for you Bobby
And I know that it's been hard
But my eyes can't see the glory
Of your bloody-minded God

I think Jesus Christ may have been an O.K. guy
I just don't have any time for his Daddy
I think Jesus Christ may have been real cool and high
But I think that God the Father was a baddie

I love the baby Jesus
Underneath the Christmas tree
But his heavy-handed father
Is the one that worries me

When he gave to the world his only 'gotten son
To be truly crucified for all us sinners
Does it say anywhere he consulted holy mum
He was hers as well as his just for beginners

I'm sorry for you Bobby
And I know what you've been through
As a rock star and a legend
And a lover and a Jew

But don't preach to me that God is love and joy
And tell me I should try to do his bidding
'Cause he told Abraham to kill his little boy
And then he said, 'Naw, I was only kidding'

And I hear you sing Bobby
Of this God you gotta serve
And I know the record's selling
But I think you lost your nerve

And I'm always gonna listen
To the changes you record
But my eyes can't see the glory
of your bloody-minded Lord

# THE MORE IT CHANGES

Old Victor's back from Tucson
A graduate of EST
He knows the latest gossip
He always buys the best
He's got the latest habit
He drops the latest name
It seems the more it changes
The more it stays the same

And Carol's back with Simon
They're like two turtle doves
Some day he's going to kill her
Perhaps that's what she loves
She's never going to end it
She can't resist his game
It seems the more it changes
The more it stays the same

My consciousness is rising
At least I'm on the way
And when my fate makes me suffer
I know what not to say
But still my mental landscape
Is covered with your name
It seems the more it changes
The more it stays the same

The world goes right on drifting
The end is still at hand
Perhaps things will be different
The day the Martians land
They may regard this planet
As wilderness to tame
If they get stuck in traffic
They've got themselves to blame
It seems the more it changes
The more it stays the same

# IT ISN'T SUCH A BAD LIFE AFTER ALL

After all the sunshine and the rain
After all the pleasure and the pain
Seems to me I really can't complain
And it isn't such a bad life after all

After all the star-dust and the rainbows
After all the suppers and the songs
After all the lovely music makers
It seems to me that nothing's really wrong
And it isn't such a bad life after all

Why was I so frightened
To have you by my side
Convinced that love was tragic
Can it be that all those poets lied?

After all the uppers and downers
Cloudy days when I was sore distressed
After all the laughter and the lovers
It seems to me that I've been truly blessed

No it's not a sad life
When all is said and done
The load keeps getting lighter
And I'll admit I've had a lot of fun

After all the weekends in the country
Knowing kids and flowers face to face
After all these travels I've decided
This planet is a fine and pleasant place
It seems to me I've reached a state of grace
And it isn't such a bad life after all

# DON'T FORGET ABOUT ME

As long as the earth keeps on spinning round
And the rivers run into the sea
Give to each man what his heart desires
And please don't forget about me

They say you're the one who gives orders, Lord
And your treasure can never be spent
So let the man who is hungry for power
Rule till his heart is content

As long as the earth keeps on spinning round
Show the killers how sweet life can be
Give to the coward a horse to ride
And please don't forget about me

Look after the leaders of East and West
Give them patience and humour as well
Don't let them make any foolish moves
And blow our nice planet to hell

I want to believe in your goodness Lord
If there's nothing that you cannot give
Hold back the hand of the suicide
And give him the wisdom to live

Let all of the lovers be satisfied
And let all the poor prisoners go free
See that the generous get a break
And please don't forget about me